THE PSYCHOPATHOLOGY OF EVERYDAY LIFE: POEMS

THE PSYCHOPATHOLOGY OF EVERYDAY LIFE: POEMS

LINDA A.W. BRAKEL

International Psychoanalytic Books (IPBooks)
New York • http://www.IPBooks.net

The Psychopathology of Everyday Life: Poems

Published by IPBooks, Queens, NY
Online at: www.IPBooks.net

ISBN: 978-1-956864-40-3

For Arthur, my own true love.

CONTENTS

CONTENTS

Section I: Relationships

Rubber Band Balls

Balls-One and Two:
Wrapped up rubber bands.
Reds in greens, greens in blues
Interwoven strands.
We three played
Chaotic bouncy path,
Pleasure
No higher math.

Dad once told me, firm but kind,
"Put that ball away."
Ball-One was whom he gestured toward,
I took him from the stove
Stowed him, firmly kindly, in his sock drawer home.

Inside same sock drawer, Ball Two
Smiled, glints of malice in her gaze.
I took her out and placed her
Where Ball One had lain.

Minutes passed, my father saw
What grown-up eyes would see:
That ball atop the stove.
My father's tone was angry,
His face grew red and hot:

"Look here girl, I see that ball,
It hasn't moved at all!"
"No you don't
I put that ball away
Exactly as you asked."

In my room. We found Ball One
Asleep, and snug, and warm
Among my socks,
Old unpaired,
And new ones, not yet worn.

My father,
Not sure what he felt, nor
Me, my state of mind:

Family,
Like twin rubber band balls,
Hard to fathom—
In token and in kind.

Father's Daughter

My father saw his childless daughter pregnant.
Tender days they were, no three of us suspecting
That inside me nestled whom he longed for:
A grandchild, one he'd never have nor had.

Life delivers scores of sadness, tens of woe,
Yet finds the soil, encodes, unfolds, and grows
Life endeavors, strives —alive alive-o.
But some lives best unlived, unknown.

They say I am indeed my father's daughter.
They say this in a kind and unkind way.
I meant to have no children, and I have none.
But my father saw me pregnant those few days.

Family Likenesses

A life or two ago
My parents, on a visit
Came to shop with us.

Bought stuff enough for four:
Leafy greens, and cookies,
Fish, and frozen juice,
Lettuce, cukes, and mustard.
Dish detergent too.

I was proud of them, my parents,
Though now I'm not sure why.

Twenty years (and more) they tried:
To do what's right, if not best
Consistent, if not wise.

Now.
The check-out clerk
Asked: "Your parents?"
My answer (was my hope):
"Do we look alike?"

"You're all short. But nope"

Ashes, Ashes

I had a Dad
Who was a man
Who is a man
No more.

A long, long life
World War strife
Work, wife, kids.
Long Island town.
And now he's under ground.

He was my Dad.
He is my Dad.
My father evermore.

Ashes, ashes.
We all fall
Down.

I Resent You More Than Love You

Beige towel, still fluffy, with no tears or rents
I see you
Feel you
Use you
And yet...
I resent
That you still work,
While
My father cannot.

Demented,
He agitates
For his release
From "Balfour"
Old age prison.
Dad thinks Denver's "The East".

* * * * * * * *

So too for those tall octagonal glasses
Elegant liquids in their confines.
Comfort my lips; cool not cold.
My mother
Bought them
Brought them home
But how can they be here
When she's gone eight years?

They're just transparent sand,
Easily broken.
"Be careful" she'd scold.

Humans and glass grow differently old?

* * * * * * *

When I was eight
I loved a dog: Flash from Flanders.
Tiny black poodle,
Ten years old.
They wanted pictures of me and Flash.
"Please don't, No!"

How to explain
The outrage
At knowing
The next time we visited
Flash would be gone.
Only the photo'd remain.

Aunt Daphne is a Paragon

Daphne is a paragon.
She's an octoroon. Maybe.
Two almost-facts, which may/may not be related.
But wait! I've looked up "octoroon"
First definition:
"An offensive term for a person with one black great-grandparent,
     no other black ancestors."
Why and how is this sweet-sounding count term
Offensive?

Being in the dark, darkens the story.
Aunt Daphne's colorful origins might be deeper than octoroon.
Maybe she's a quadroon: three white grandparents, the other black.
Is "quadroon" more or less offensive?

If you and I are ignorant about X,
Do we know more or less about X
Together than
Alone?

My octoroon makes macaroons.
She's an octagon, at least.
Only Daphne still calls me "Lindy."
I like that about her
And me.

Nevermore

I had a friend
The best of friends
Who is a friend
No more.

She said of "friend"
(The term we use)
We use it
Way too widely.

She said we ought
To put more thought
To whom
The term applies.

But now she's my ex-friend
She's my best friend naught.

Subway Love I

Head in a book
Head in his lap
Two bodies, three lives
Headed uptown.

Godspeed?
No. Not even close.
Slower, faster
Subway steed.

Intractable tracks
Intractable course.
Stories still unfolding
Still
Unknown.

I Know Her Only By These Outward Signs

Bald head
Male?
No, female.
Fashion?
No, Chemo.

She is
Walking
Walking
Walking

Crossing paths with us

Walking
Walking
Walking
With our dog.

* * * * * * *

There's a tree stump
On her verge
Very flat
Very large.
Two strides long
I stomp on it
Every day

Every weekday all year long
Then it is gone.

So was her car
Obama & Biden 2008
DEU 1202 (Mon Dieu!)
Subaru

My Love, My Editor

He can't keep his hands off
    The editor's pen
He crosses out ~~all~~ most that I've said.
But he can't keep his hands off
    The body I own
He approves of ~~most~~ all that I am.

Subway Love II

First lovers
The Two that were One
Inseparable, until
She left him.
He threw himself on a
Subway track...
Train!
One leg gone.
Two that were One =
One + Some irrational fraction.
No whole numbers remain.

Double Bed

It is hard to tell
Where you start
From
Where I end
Tangled as we are
In
Double Bed

Section II: States of Mind are States of Body

Frogkick Feet

In the Olympics, a swimmer I'd be.
Done some running, but it's not for me.
My feet turn out, there's a technical name.
Never could ice skate, though I've always been game;
Nor ride water skis; well that's not quite true.
Once up

   My   pulled through.
     feet   always
       make   I'm
          a   and
            V

On a path at college some wag "mocked" my gait.
Turns out his feet turned out too—our mutual fate.
We didn't get married and have lots of kids.
No, I out-toed my way--he out-toed his.

Back to the sports world
A recent report
Held that years of the frog kick would force normal feet out.
Breaststrokers frog kick; that's my very best feat,
Breaststroking faster than most freestylers I meet.
Yes, turn defect to a win, that'd make a nice story.
Yes, imagine my getting Olympic size glory!

Ah, but my talent is far from elite.
Yet I do a mean breaststroke,
I've got frogkick feet.

Merry Ontario

My conference colleagues
All so grim.
    I'm too serious too.

We give our papers: ponderous,
Technical insights,
    With much too much ado.

After the meeting
Sad, without flair,
The doors to the building say
Warning: please don't skateboard
Down or up the stairs.

In sweltering heat
We also find
A band of kids
Cavorting
In furry
Masks and hides.

They've been studying for 100 days
At—The Mascot College of Greater Ontari...
O, these people know life's ways
The training-mascot practice was
The lesson best
Brought
Home.

Paranoids Are Always Right

Paranoids are always right
Hypochondriacs, never wrong.
I sing with inner tempo
A driving walking song.

I count the dogs, the birds, the cars—
The cheating VW brand.

Then, someone's behind me.

Zeno, halving distances, distances and space.
He's always just halfway, never apace.
This paradox I can't believe
Though mightily I try.

So just in case I rev it up
Speed-walk walking pace.
A chase is underway.

I don't turn back
I pour it on
My follower undeterred.

When finally, at last, at last,
I risk—a brisk—look back:

My stalker's of a different race.

Not a human
Not a mammal
Not a bird

It's my own blue backpack.
Moving as I move.

Half And Half-not

You can have my right hand

          if I can keep my left.

          I'll take my left arm too

The right will go to you.

You can have my right foot
its leg and ankle too.

          The left'll stay with me clear up past
          my knee.

Likewise for the girdles, both the pelvic and the shoulder
They divide quite nicely, left, right, one half for each holder.
No trouble with the eyes, ears, kidneys, lungs, and genitalia,
Even stomach, small intestine, spine may split without much
          failure.

We're symmetrical   Except when we are not.

      Now divide my brain, my soul, my heart.

Race Matters

*A Villanelle For Delano Meriwether, M.D., hematology-oncology
physician and world class sprinter*

"Yes, I can do that. Impresses the hell out of me."
Said Dr. Meriwether, watching Olympics on TV.
Race is a concept; race is a race, with winners and losers galore.

But races are contests you can win too.
"Yes, I can do that. Impresses the hell out of me."
Said I, Dr. Brakel, intense, engaged, in "constructing" poetry.

My brother, a lonely, *happy?* man
With troubles so great that he "knows"
Race is a concept; race is a race, with losers and losers galore.

"Impresses the hell out of me."
"I can't do that," is all he said,
My family's great divide.

When did I realize, when did I know,
Race is a concept; race is a race, with winners and losers galore?
When Delano triumphed in seventy-four?

The date was 1972 in fact.
Heme-onc doctor, 100 yard dash, way ahead of the pack.
Yes, he could do that. Impresses the hell out of me.
Race is a concept; race is a race, with winners and losers galore.

Bent

Paper clips are bent, they have two curls.
Dogs asleep are fuzzy, fur-lined swirls.
Mine beside me, clockwise, right side out
Awakens startled this time due to naught.

Folded-up, a man goes down steep stairs.
He must proceed with caution, lots of care,
Suffers his diseased nerves.
When did he have a young man's verve?

Pity I can't quell.
For him for me or both? How to tell?
When dogs have three legs
Or when they're lame
They look plucky,
I sense no shame.

Tripod dogs like paper clips bent straight
Have lost their norm, yet motate free, no self-hate.

The Y and the Funeral Home

The YMCA and the Funeral Home
Face across the street.
Stairmasters, treadmills, rowing machines
Time and death compete.

Stately mansion, wrought iron fences,
A well-appointed hearse.
In our city's planning
Which came first?

As the winter light grew poor
The funeral parlor pallor
More ghastly than before.
Then against the fence I saw

A snowman in a cape.
His days were numbered
Much as yours and mine.
But that dark and snowy night,
Life and death felt fine.

Omentum

Death, I no longer care
About my dog's feelings,
My neighbors' distress,
Nor YMCA member, Louisa,
Laid to rest.

Freud's "de-cathexis", indifference in grey.
And in secret small steps, more mounted each day
Mounting, accruing like cells with mutations
Till all active thought trains fell from their stations.

Not that it's painful
Not that it's sad.
Just that it's tiny, angstrom size, small
Just that it's nothing, nothing at all.

Momentum, omentum, an omen, a curse
Omentum, momentum, a fever, a life—death even worse.

Know-It-Alls Can Be Deceived

Know-it-alls can be deceived,
Culture critics too.

Red state type,
His black & blue tattoo.

On his deltoid
The left, near his heart.

It's intricate and bizarre,
A grotesque portraiture

With bench presses and curls
 In sync with every grunt and groan.

His infant daughter's face
The baby's mouth contorts

What secret vow possessed him,
Debasing her like that?

She'll be grown up soon enough,
His deltoid turned to fat.

The picture faded, warped,
She'll be a different girl.

Then I see some numbers,
Part of the tattoo:

Her birthday date,
Repeated
Her death date too.

Errant Heart

with thanks to Sherman Alexie for "Crazy Horse Boulevard"

I used to think
    Because I am
        A white baby-boomer Jew
        Educated, wealthy
        Happily married
        Female (Cis-gendered)
        Living with husband and dog—
        (A Whippet mix they say.)

I'd have nothing of interest to write.

I used to think that
    Until I read
        "Crazy Horse Boulevard"
        An imposing poem, I'd say, by
        A Spokane Indian, Gen Xer
        Educated, wealthy,
        Happily married
        Male (Cis-gendered),
        Wife and Children—
        (Two boys.)

* * * * * * * * * * * * * * *

This poem is nothing like his.

This poem is about looking right then left

Or looking left then right.

    Cross streets only after looking left and right.
    Perform clandestine acts—say, public bra removal—after
        checking left and right.
    Contemplate your med school classmates to the left and to
        the right
    Half'll drop out, Half that half gone
    Before anybody understands "iatrogenic".

This poem is also about children in hospitals.

    Pediatrics ward, Columbia Presbyterian
    Look left,
    Boy with leukemia
    1959—no cure.
    Farther left,
    Girl who could not feel pain.
    No advantage,
    My Uncle, the young doctor whispers,
    "She'll soon be dead.".

As for me
Simple surgery
Will fix
My troubled heart
And I'll be fine.

1960, Lennox Hill,
The pre-op room, a cozy two.
Look left:
Big Deb, bad rheumatic heart.
If I synchronize my breath with hers
Our fates will intertwine.
I fear.

* * * * * * * * * * * * * * *

Surgery took no time
For me, but not the clock.

Recovery room, each painful breath
Fact, fact, fact, fact
Left upper ribs, bent, almost cracked.
My breath, every inspiration,
A moanful rhyme.
        The nurse
        Pointed left and said:
        "Patty's not moaning.
        Her operation was worse than yours."

My errant heart.
    And I
    Kept moaning, flush
    With satisfaction
    Patty will die soon
    I will not.

I used to think

Conversation in the Pediatrics Ward

"I think I'm dying. I want a pony.
My legs, they still feel numb."
"You're not dying. We'll get you a pony.
This Christmas will be fun."
The room, already cold, fell silent.
Cold and metallically bare.

The mother sighed, quietly weeping.
The father stared at the dripping IV.
The son breathed harder and faster and deeper,
Rasping the truth he already knew:

"Things fall from the sky. I see sparkly stars,
Bursting inside my eyes."
"Yes, stars can fall, so can rockets and moons
But they rise up again at dawn."
"No Mom. You're wrong. We're not going home.
I'm not. I know that for sure."
The boy's breaths grew faster, more shallow, and then
    Stopped.
But started rapid again. He no longer talked, just cyclically
    breathed,
For hours, four hours, his last.

Then said his mom, to the son who was gone, her voice as blue as the
    sky
"I'll miss you in summer.
I'll miss you in Spain.
I'll miss you with snow on the ground.
I'll miss you tomorrow.
I'll miss you in May.
I'll miss you till I am no more."

The father then said to the room and his wife, his voice grave as a
    grave
"I'd have got him a pony,
I'd have shown him the ropes,
How to shave and woo him a wife.
I'd have played games with him,
Maybe hockey or chess,
Taught him to scale fish with a knife."

Things fall from the sky
Stars, rockets, and moons.
They don't resurrect.
Sons die.

The History of Anatomy

It was dresses they made in the Kneeland St. building,
    Where we cut bodies, one cadaver for five.
It was wages they worked for in the Kneeland St. building,
    Where we are the students of body part secrets, keeping humans
    alive.
It was hot in the summer and cold in the winter with lighting from
dim to despair.
    Where for us it is freezing, cold corpses the reason,
    formaldehyde scent in the air.
It was sewing machines and cutting machines, no dead space at all
in that room.
    Where for us it is bodies wherever we gaze; all dead space, all
    dead space, no sound.

How can I learn this?
How can I not?
How can I just endure
    The smell and the cold and the cold hard fact
    that the body's no body, no more.

A Metaphor Died on My Watch

For Jaak Panksepp (1943-2017) affective neuroscience pioneer

A metaphor died on my watch
    Today.
I killed a centipede cleanly.
Drowning, viz. a watery death, uniquely
    Unappealing.
Blunt blow. Centipede down! From the waiting room
    Ceiling.
Oh that sentient centa-legged one
He's gone.
    One waits.
    One laughs.
    One tickles rats.
    Similes die as soldiers.
    Their clocks have stopped.
    Their ticks have Lyme's
    Your lime's still green,
While the man who tickled rats
Is gone.
Lymphoma.
The rats, they laughed, but not at Jaak.
They laughed. We couldn't hear them.
They laughed, appalled at us, perhaps.

Murine mirth.

Us/Cancer Center

We went together, Ira and I.
    The drugs
        dripped
        dripped
        dripped
        dripped
    into Nancy.

She slept. He and I
Watched her sleep.
I read the newspaper. Ira
Watched her sleep.
Ira did some errands. I
Watched her sleep.
Ira came back. We
Watched her sleep,
I went home. He stayed and
Watched her sleep.

Then they went home.

    * * * * * * * * * * * * * * * * * *

Nancy had cancer for
Four, maybe five
Years.

Her symptoms:
    Nausea, vomiting,
    hair loss, weakness,
    fatigue, cramping,
    easy bruising, opportunistic infections

All from the
Treatment.

      * * * * * * * * * * * * * * * * * *

The center is
Cozy, homey, decorated
In warm, understated
Light blue checked curtains and hardy,
Not pretty plants.

Down the hall essays and pictures
Done by children
Who are also
Cancer patients.

One picture is called:
"My Cancer Center"
It isn't "My Cancer's Center"
This center does not make cancers comfortable.

      * * * * * * * * * * * * * * * * * *

There are four kinds of people there:
    patients,
    medical staff,
    family,
    friends.

Membership
changes with time.
Four types collapse
Into one.

We'll all be
In our cancer center,
Which is why
We   try
To   feel

At home.

Section III: Nations, States, Cities

An Idea, A Failed Poem, Then Another Poem

It came to me in a flash—an analogy—three parts no sequence. Yet, to explain requires separate descriptions: First, a feeling of superiority as I noted that our neighbors' house had a basement window with no glass or screen. (Our house suffers from disregard rather than disrepair.) Next, realizing that this opening constitutes an open invitation for squirrels, opossums, mice, racoons, and chipmunks, it was clear that these neighbors would have to move all of their animal-control operations inside. Our external policing includes not only proper basement windows and walls with no holes, but also a small animal-chasing (and occasionally catching/eviscerating) multi-breed rescue dog. Finally, the analogy: Yes, stop them from outside or inside. True for border crossings. Squirrels and other animals not wanted inside. "No" to bad microbes.

Attempts to control human migration are in the news every day. As I have nothing to add but my sorrow, I'll move on to squirrels and other animals designated as pests when they appear in our domiciles. As far as external measures, along with windows and walls without holes, and menacing dogs, squirrels and their lot can be shot.

> I knew a man I called a friend
> Who shot-to-kill
> Woodpeckers pecking
> His ultra-modern wooden house.

We weren't friends and this doesn't fit because the birds were not attempting to enter his home, merely doing their woodpecker job, but it does demonstrate another external control measure.

Third part of the analogy: Medical advances have refined both external and internal management of bad microbes. Here are some external operations: netting, screens (without holes) to prevent various microbial vectors, e.g. mosquitoes; quarantines of animals, human and otherwise; high tech measures including sneezing into one's elbow, and obsessive-compulsive hand washing. Mixed inside/outside measures include improvements in host defensive conditions. Vaccines boost specific immune defenses—tiny walls of cellular attackers defend against an early offensive mission.

The inside game—antibiotics. They kill the good microbes too, but that's an idea (and maybe a failed poem) for another time. But of issue here is the most important mode of action of the most common class of antibiotics. All antibiotics stop bacterial growth. Some interfere with bacterial protein metabolism. Others prevent bacterial replication by damaging their DNA. But by far the most significant means by which antibiotics work is by making it impossible for bacteria to properly construct their own cell walls!

I tried to write a striking poem about this trio: "alien" people, animal "pests," and "bad" microbes—this is how you stop them.
But the walls spiraled—
So, instead I wrote the following poem:

This is how you stop them

People! All you "non-us" types, The Wall shall be built just for you.
The Wall will keep you *bad* ones out and the *good* ones too.
A national matter from our nation's mad hatter, his hatred
Will splatter his perfect tall wall. Let's build it of
Lettuce, let's see if he'll let us, remaining
Unpicked, his white un-pick-ed fence.
All white. Alt Right. All right?

There, Then, Here, Now: A Villanelle

What kind of country do we have here,
Where *Giants kill Pirates* again and again?
What can it mean? He wondered, he feared.

He came to New York, bereft of all cheer
Having fled the Nazis, '36 it was then.
"What kind of country have they there?"

Everyone asked. The answer was clear.
Jews get out, go away—while you still can!
What did it mean? They wondered, they feared.

Real Pirates today, no rings in their ears.
Policemen kill Blacks, both children and men
What kind of country have we here?

I raise up my arms, both hands in the air.
Don't shoot! I protest—saves me, but not them.
What does this mean? We wonder, we fear.

My protest, my gesture, impotent red flare
The killing goes on—spilled blood, black men.
What kind of country have we here?
What does this mean? We wonder, we fear.

Walking on a Sarasota Beach
on a Sunny Wednesday

(XY)
Bow legged ex-why

(XY))XX(
Alongside
Knock kneed double-ex

In sex
She surrounds him
) (XY) (

11 11 11 11
Children, they had four
All had legs, two and straight

Regression to the mean?
Yes, and progression.

Lost Cities Sonnet: Good Bye East Stroudsburg

Uncle Kurt was 98, never 99.
A pity?
We drove to Stroudsburg East
Two hours from the city.

We grew old. He grew older.
"We" became a different lot.
The Poconos stood, unfazed,
To our family twists and plots.

We said "so long" to Uncle Kurt.
We'd bid Aunt Sarah adieu.
But I never thought, East Stroudsburg,
We were saying goodbye to you.

Betty died, farewell to Phoenix; Mom is gone, so Pittsburgh too.
Seattle, Spokane are you lost next, the next time we pass through?

In Guadalajara Drug Lords Don't Take The Bus

Thigh to thigh to thigh to thigh.

Back to front

Front to back

Too tight to move

No room to steal

No way to run.

Instead,

We pass our fare up, person-by-person, to the driver

We pass the change back, person-by-person to the rider.

Humanity's triumph

On the bus in Guadalajara.

Mexico City Haikus

<u>Impulse Thwarted in a Mexico City Restaurant</u>

Why should I straighten

a t_ilted fine f_{au}x Kah_lo

Nature's art. Let it go.

<u>A Starbucks Confusion: Happily Ever NAFTA</u>

"¿Café con leche?"

Mexico, Starbucks infused.

"¿Qué? ¡Oh! ¡Latte!"

<u>Two Haikus on Two Ozone Action Days in Mexico City</u>

Surrounding mountains

We cannot see you because

Smog defiles the air

* *

Cars we drive. And cars

We value. Modern life can't stop.

Mountains, do you care?

Veracruz Haikus

Veracruz has life!

Cockroaches, many

But today, no mosquitoes.

No Zika! Hurray!

Monolingual English Speaker's Double Haiku

No Spanish for me

I am so monolingual.

But in Veracruz

No English is used.

I am speechless but happy

For Spanish to thrive.

Section IV: States of Nature

New Growth Green

Every day, as I walk by, I note a house, uncertain green.
    Pea soup green but not as murky,
    Mint green but not as light,
    Forest green but not as forthright,
    Kelly green but not as bright.
Why would someone choose this color?
How could people love this hue?
Then one day in not-yet-Spring.
Flush against the house grew stubble,
    Coiling softly up and out.
Fuzz and house—
New Growth Green.
    Not yet finished,
    Not yet tired,
    Not yet full,
    Hardly formed, but therefore thrilling,
Thoughts and worlds renewed.

A First Love Leaves in Summer

Summer is an empty time
To fill your head
And wait
For fuller times.

Two Mammals, Full Fall

My dog's black and white.
She curls down beside me,
Muzzle in knee.

Greys shine through the colors;
Clouds through the walls.
Background for colors,
Colors for dogs.

We breathe and read together,
Drawing too much in, inside.
Air with no color,
Worlds in words, black and white.

Mood falls softly,
Cushioned not by leaves or clouds.
But the season is full,
And so are our lungs.

Winter Ice

Which is the harder feat
To walk on eggshells? Or
On water?

Just walking is hard.
But only if you think about it.

Eggshells are hard
To break
End to end
With bare hands
But easy with bare feet.

* * * * * * * *

To stay married
Walk on eggshells
Make omelets
Break eggs.

As for walking on water—
The Basilisk Lizard can,
And Brazilian Pygmy Geckos,
And Water Striders,
And two kinds of Grebes,
And Storm Petrels.

So can Jesus
Me too
When it freezes.

Not Half Done

Look man look!
Twigs like a frog
A frog in two dimensions.
Black and small
No depth at all
No skin of green
Not moist, no sheen.

It is a frog
It *was* a frog
It's not a frog-like fresco.

Let's move on
We've work to do
Our days not half done.

Death's neglected
Life goes on
Right foot follows left.

But on my left
A bird is dead
A Robin
Red breast sullied.

And on my right
My neighbor's plant,
A broken green lobelia,
Still stands up
But not straight up
Sad right angle bent.

Small red flowers venture out
But death is on the way.
Death will have its way
Alright
With birds
With plants
With bodies.

But ho!
A rabbit springs.
Flashy fleet display
Life's silent power play.

Modern Travel

From the air the earth
Is sculpted
On a flat 2-D.
Plane

Colors demark
Geo-boundaries
Laughing at officious
Marks of State.

Green agri-circles touch fertile squares.
Fallow fields look richly brown.
Lakes, dots of limpid blue.
Rivers flow, we know
But seem so still.

* * * * * * * *

From a car this vast land,
Grand, expansive, breathless.
Then majesty begets monotony;
Monotonous majesty
We endure.

Mustang Mountains

Mustang Mountains
We can't tame you.
Being human
We will try.
Snow-capped words
And craggy concepts
Tools for climbing
Minerals mined.

You'll be here
While we'll be dying.
Not you,
But we
Will wonder
Why?

Section V: Dogs

Dog School

Do dogs know they'll die?
People know;
Each dog. Every dog.
Will I?

Then there's Dog School

"Will Andy's teacher be a dog?"
Asked little Riva when
Her first dog, Andy,
Enrolled in Dog School.
"No! Lassie won't be at the Blackboard
She won't have chalk or a laser pointer
And no polished dog bones.
People teach Dog School."

But dogs learn from dogs.
Our dog, Jet Ann, learned to jump
Our four foot fence
From her next-door
Siberian Husky, Ski.

Dog Schools are not fish schools
No orderly silent gliding.
No flock behavior at free play time.
Instead, unchoreographed interactions
Only dogs understand:

Dog A with Dog B; Dog B with Dog C; Dogs D & E with Dog A.
Too complex for people.

Dog Schools are co-ed.
Dogs and their humans relearn
Our cooperative bond.

Unanswerable questions
Are wrong questions,
So philosophers say.
Dog School
Teaches
Questions about death
Are wrong questions.
At least for now.

Woof!

Like Fixedly Watching?

Like fixedly watching
Rivers flow?
H_2
Bonds
To
Big fat O
Same same
Same same?
No no
No!

She's a watch dog, Dog
No, not by breed
Rapt
Attentive
To our street:
The postperson (I know, "worn out trope")
A dog
A cat
A squirrel
Two birds

Mundane to me
But hey!
I'm the kind who stares at words.

My Dog and My Book

To her it is a neutral thing.
Its blue and white hard backed cover--
Not something she'd ever judge it by.
She likely sees the printed name—mine,
And its title:
The Ontology of Psychology.

But she sees not a name, not a title, not print at all.
She sees black marks, lots of them, if she's looking at all.
Maybe she smells my past sweat, exuded
As I toiled to write this tome
This smell would be familiar to her,
But no, this is not what she smells,
Not now.

The thing smells of now.
The desk, the room
The dust that has made this book its home.
That's my dog's
Ontology of Psychology.

Jet's Dream

with appreciation to "Jet Stream"

The bird flies out of my head
An idea flies out of my mind
Into the world.
The idea-bird takes flight
Dividing my mind
Not evenly.

The mouse sits on the dining room chair
At table's head.
"You aim too high," the mouse intones
Flinging ideas, avian style
Out and into the universe of giants.

Dogs can't drive
But in dreams they do.
My sweetest canine, Jet Ann
In the driver's seat
In chaotic traffic
Driving our car.

I try to save her
With all that I own,
With all that I am.
But I am in the backseat
I can't reach the steering wheel,
I can't reach Jet.

My arms too short
My aims too tall.

Astray In Oxford—A Sonnet

At a launderette, wash undone
We saw a dog, like our Jet Ann.
Though sad he was, he ventured forth,
Black and White, Head and Tail Face down.

An unclaimed dog
Let's call him X
A dog alone
Untethered.

A dog who surely sleeps outdoors
In cold
In rain
In weather.

But X was not alone, that day
His person came; two sad strays.

Dogs In Spring

The pit bull next door
Is Nina.
Her human's name—
Alexandra, I think.
Nina and Alexandra
Lovely names.
Lovely Nina—white with spots of brown.
Exuberant. She jumps.
Alexandra struggles
To control her,
To contain her,
But agrees with me:
Nina's a charmer.

* * * * * * *

Our Xenia ("X" pronounced as "Z")
Nina's next-door neighbor.
A rescued greyhound or whippet mix:
Beautiful brindle
Brown and white.

* * * * * * *

Abandoned pup
In cardboard box
Along a Kentucky highway.
Was her mother sad?

* * * * * * *

Xenia
Fast and anxious.
Fast and sweet.
Fast and smart.
Fast and devious.
Fast!

* * * * * * *

Sudden Spring
On backyard decks.
Nina and Xenia sun themselves
Dogs in the sun
Sun Dogs.

Our Dog is a Hunter (Not a Voyeur)

Our dog is a hunter
She's stealthy sly
Constructing blinds and ruses.
    Resting
    Resting
    Resting
Until she bounds and pounces!

Eleven years with us
A dozen squirrels she's captured.
But in these juicy days of June
She's possessed, enraptured.

Aware she cannot reach them,
Aware of the fence,
Aware of the trees and the railings,

She cannot take her eyes from them,
Squirrel sexual mores and wailings.

She's witnessed our sex a thousand times
Or more, I doubt she's counting.
But mammalian sex of the human kind
Holds no interest for our canine.

"It's boring" I can hear her say.
"Where's the chase before the mounting?"

Bloodhound

Because of children
Blood-drawing areas have pictures:

Raccoons, baboons,
Cats, no rats, no bats,
Giraffes, and bears, and seals.
Black and white stallions
To show power and verve
But a cancer resistant,
Protected protector,
The elephant, would better serve.

Why not a bloodhound, a trusty big bloodhound on every clinical wall?
They're big, they're bold, they're beautiful, "well behaved",
Not baying whenever they chose.

They're good at scents,
At tracking things
Things, we people lose.
Still, if I should lose myself, or you,
Whatever I would want...
Even a bloodhound...cannot.

* * * * * * * * * * * * * * * * * * * *

Blackie

When I was small I had a dog.
Blackie was his name.
He was brown and soft,
Made of cloth,
Thereby rather tame.

I lost him in a freezer case.
It was 1952.
When he was lost,
I was too.
Nothing felt the same.

We looked for him,
We really did,
But all to no avail.
I needed a bloodhound,
A trusty big bloodhound.

He might have been mostly black, but
Named Brownie just the same.

I can't remember
It doesn't matter
It comes to mind just now.
I have a neighbor,
An actual neighbor,

She's a bloodhound strong and true.
She bays when she wants to,
She wants to a lot
As people and dogs pass through.

I don't know her person
He doesn't know me.
Friendly, we are not.
But I did want to know her,

This beautiful bloodhound.
So, I asked her name.
"Blackie" he said, no smile at all,
Despite her deep brown coat.

I smiled inside and outside too
A cosmic joke,
A feel good feel,

Joy can be inane.

Montana Dogs

I. Lolo Mountain Dog

In Lolo Forest
Brooks babble green splashed blues,
Against craggy rocks, browns and tans.
Evergreen trees,
The Montana Big Sky Blue.

We chose the shortcut.
Mountain pass?

The grey scrub brush
Scraped our rented Chevrolet,
Dust rose up to hide its pea green paint.
.

The unpaved road split into many
Forks with no markers. We took
This tine this time, and that tine next.
We pulled a fallen tree off
The road to
Pass.

Quiet desperation.

"Roads go up, and over, and down, don't they?"

A tossed beer can lightened my heart.
Indifferent worldly nonchalance once again.
And the road pointed down.
We headed down.
Our spirits climbed.

A dog.

We stopped.
Black and tan, male,
Basset body and damaged eye,
Not sad, empty,
Starving, surprised.
We offered him crackers but
He would not come close,
Much less ride with us.

Of his former life,
His collar, tags
Intact, but out of reach.
We couldn't read them,
Nor name him anew,

A Lolo Mountain dog
For life.

Diminished
We went on.

II. Smiley

He was fat and happy
Well-fed and clean
A collar—no tags.
A dog on the Whitefish golf course, barking,
As each self-important golfer addressed
His white round self-representation
And addressed it again, in the rough:
"Is that me? No, it must be you. I'm a Ram Tour 1."

The dog came with us.
On hole #14
He bounded over the hills we trudged,
Smiling.

Brown and white,
Unlikely shape,
Half dingo, half Rottweiler pup.
On hole #15
He lay, submitting, paws up too.
Barked only at the foursome behind.
"Can't we take Smiley home with us?"

He smiled again on hole #16
A Cheshire smile--
And
Was
Gone.

III. Logan

We climbed up Big Mountain.
Old ones and young ones took the gondola
To the top and walked down.
We hiked steeply up.

On their way down
Old ones and young ones delighted
At mountain lakes and flowers
Even as they strained to foot-plant.
They greeted us
Mentioned climbers ahead:
A man, a woman, a dog.

Logan, the Yorkshire terrier,
Trail leader, led us up.
When we passed his people
His tags tinkled merrily
Until his group called him back,
Picked him up.
We climbed on ahead.

From the summit we watched them descend—
A spritely springy speck
Dancing in front
Of two bigger forms
Logan, unburdened by the human condition.

Section VI: Other (Non-Human) Animals

Crow Sonnet

Assembled in tall trees of autumn, they're
An army, no an air force, all in black.
So many, the colored leaves, now in wing-ed stacks,
Crow clouds reach up through branches, fill the air.

They're always bigger than you think, I aver,
Their calls of caw and caw again so loud
Impressive, so expressive, I'd be proud
Were I to take to sky and be that bird.

So hard to be a raven, you're so smart.
Your kinship ties we humans cannot know.
Yet resting coal black feathers on bright snow,
You all embody nature's starkest art.

The trees you crows command, how do you choose
Why always cemetery-trees near tombs?

Crow Haiku

Awoke today to
Hear then see black swarms of crows
On crow-top-ed trees

Fox Haiku

I go outside and
Hope to see a fox atop
Our fox top-ed tree.

Lullaby For Lions

Look for zebras when you've looked for horses
But there were no horses found.
Look for zebras when you're hunting and hungry
But quickly and don't make a sound.

For once the herd is in motion
The black white black commotion
Will make it appear
Not a singleton here
But rather a zebra-mass ocean.

Yet you could get lucky and snare
A hooved and multi-striped beast.
Then in due course your deepest desires
Will turn to rest, from feast.
With bones and stripes—in a heap
Lion-eyes seek not prey, but sleep.

When this obtains
From all striped ones abstain—
Count sheep!

Mrs. Frog's Lament

I had a husband green
And true.
He brought home many bugs
And flies.
And now I'm left to wonder *Why,*
Oh why?

Resourceful,
Strong and bold.
He fought off predators
Young and old.
Humans yes, and egrets too.
But now I'm left to wonder *Why,*
Oh why?

He fertilized my eggs
In style unmatched.
In warmer water
He watched them hatch.
A lot of them from tadpoles
Grew to handsome frogs like him.

Frog wives we knew were green
With envy
At my great good luck.

My frog mate could
With great prowess
Propagate genes and
No less
Enfold me in his smooth caress
In waters warm or cold.

So why did he leave me?
And our kids?
Why did he disappear?
I went to the po-lice.
I went to a priest.
No frog had a clue.

He had seemed happy.
He had seemed well.
In the prime of life.
Had he been murdered?
Had he been drugged?
Or had I done something wrong?

Was my skin drying?
Less green and shiny?
Were the kids too demanding?
The pond stultifying?
My mother annoying?
Our friends too damn cloying?
Too many constraints on his time?

I never found answers.
I still lament.
I sing out *Why,*
Oh why?

There's a postscript here
That's worth belief.
A fairy tale myth
No help with my grief.
About some spell upon a man
Turned into a frog
And then released
When kissed by some girl,
A Princess, I think, and
The frog became a Prince.

But my frog was a prince!
My prince of a frog
I miss him every day
I can't understand
What I can't understand
There's no moral in this tale.
Why, oh why?
I wonder anew
This, my constant
Silent wail.

Alas No Chicks

For Chip: A Cardinal, 1987-2004

A bird I know thinks he's important.
His legs are bent, he's kind of small,
But damn, he's Corvid clever.
He's light and fleet with great technique
For worm and moth ingesting.
He feints and dives with dreams of sky
While in his cage he dwells.
Females fly by; he signals them, urging them, hard sell.
Red bird blues, he sings to them; metal bars the way.
"Olinger, please" like Updike's town
(Without John's elegant words)
Importance is a relative term, more so even for birds.

Brown and White Mouse

Mouse, we know you by your leavings.
Mouse, so small and brown white trim,
A mammal, you remind me of our dog.

Mouse, we catch you in our trap.
Mouse, we have a heart we take you to
The park with trees and shrubs and grass.

Mouse, you find release confusing,
You jump, then bound through several planes.
Mouse, achingly tender,
Profound.

The Crane

With thanks to Robert Frost

The metallic giant
Dips and rises
Takes a bird's name:
Crane.

But
No fish,
No flights,
No turning back.

Philosopher Seeks A Singular Pet

In black and white on a type-set page in a scholarly text it was said:
"Moose, those two-toe ungulates, seldom make good pets."
Amusing, quite affectionate, as these antlered creatures are,
A moose-less state was suggested when pragmatics were in view.

But what of pseudopodia, say amoebas for a start?
Hmmm?...They are protean—flexible—to a fault;
Perhaps these single cellular ones would work where moose could not.
One could visit them by microscope as often as one wished.
Feeding, another non-problem, of this or that a pinch.

But there are some age-old problems pet amoebas would make worse.
(Not counting here occasioning this verse.)
Does our pet "One" live forever, dividing as amoebas do?
Or is "One's" life quite short, with "Two" and "Two" each brand new?
And is "One" the same as "Two" and "Two" in token not just kind?
Or does "Two" and "Two" from "One" make "One" tracing
    ontologically from behind?

The naming problem too is wicked, no matter how you turn.
Are both daughter cells named "Two"—or maybe "One-the-second"?
Then how to distinguish one from another, not to mention from their
    mother;
Who by the way, either infinitely exists;
Or is just the remembered primal other.

Ah let's stick to dogs and birds.
Pet-hood should be easy.
The problems with infinite pets—despite initial appeal—
Make me physio-sophically queasy.

Section VII: Concepts

Polymath Mother

I'm a polymath

Almost
But I've never arrived.
Fitting,
As I well
Believe
Ne'er do well
Equals
Near do well.

I throw well
For a girl
Equals
Not like a girl.
Fitting,
As I
Do not
"Mother"
Well.

Yes, I like his work
So much
That I
Believe
No improving on
The canvass
Equals
My non-children,
Polymaths all.

Extant King Of France

If all the hair my smooth haired dog
    has shed
Were gathered, weaved, assembled
    end to end.
Grand and elegant dog hair coats
    we'd have
To outfit all the extant
    Kings of France.

For every plant whose green
    extrusions fall
Suppose we could compress them
    one and all.
We'd have a mountain
    not of gold
A green leaf mountain,
    majestic to behold.

If common human misery could
    be summed,
Channeled, forced, enticed
    to do some work;
Those many fears and flaws,
    I'd take them home
And write the most extraordinary
    ordinary poem.

On Learning Wisk Detergent Is No More
For Donald Hall with apologies for the paraphrase

Donald Hall in sorrow said
    You will lose
    Everything
    Eventually
    If you live long.

In sorrow, yes,
    But if
    You die young
    You will lose
    Everything
    No less--
    Just fast.

Grandpa Ruby cheerfully said
    If you eat string beans
    A Hundred Years
    You'll live long.

No Way! Yes, Way

I don't like cats
I do love dogs
I saw 100 birds.
I found three bats
And two large rats
No cows, no sheep, no turds.
On second thought I made this up.
So much of this is wrong. I think I best
Begin again, as though we really could.

I am a goat, I am a lamb, I like to run and play.
I mowed the grass, I did it fast, before the rain today.
I turned it on, I worked till dawn I finished my assignment.
With a four-leaf clover, I checked it over, then sent it on its way.
It came back wet and sad and spent: a book, a poem, a journey.

But not so bad, not so fast, not so out of step
I am a man, I am a dog, I am what I am not.

So Close

Were I to cave-dwell, my echo would be strong.
On sidewalks, on sun-days, my shadow grows long.
Suppose my echo and shadow were to meet.
Could I arrange that? And where would it be?

Would they prefer to be alone?
Or would three be nice?
Could I come along?

One has a voice, follows just like mine,
The other a presence, two-dimensional line.
But the one that appears cannot hear or see,
And the echo sings out, but hears only me.

Is touch the sense that binds relations?
Light wave to sound wave, photon phonation?

But no need to rush
Echoes and shadows,
Like wishes and outcomes,
Never quite touch.

Everything Counts

Being purposeful is a thing.
Being serious too.
Aiming agentially toward something
Is something I can do.

Nothing should be wasted, everything should count:

Endless boring lectures, walking to the gym, brushing teeth, and
hair, and dog,
fine clothes on gentle spin. Cooking breakfast, packing lunch,
picking pears all day,
keeping all appointments, while on-alert for strays. Going to the
movies, sometimes all
alone, talking on the telephone with nothing much to say. Doing
taxes, learning stats,
getting a degree, painting houses, painting walls, sexual ecstasy.
Going gray and
growing bean sprouts, losing friends and more. Horseback rides,
and subtle put downs,
jackets made of wool. Yankee teams and English muffins, puffins
who can fly. AP
classes, stethoscopes, amoebas that can't die.

Great Aunt Rose had bad arthritis living in the Bronx.
Poetic license: she had psoriasis, her joints were not destroyed.
She was left-handed, they made her a righty;
Her work was ironing ties.

She lived, she worked, we visited—at 81 she died.
At the time I didn't get it, maybe I still don't,
But what I take to be instructive follows from her life.

You can't predict life's outcome, seeing what you see.
So bring to bear everything,
Though everything can change.
It helps to know you cannot know,
Its slope, its mean, its range.

Third Street

Today in black & white:

Four dogs
Four leashes
Three people
Fat father, blond daughter
Slim Black young adult: three leashes, three dogs
She laughs.
We say hello
Dogs as dogs,
Folks as folks
Freed by dogs.

Today in shades of grey:

Half a mouse:
Two hind legs,
Two small feet
Foot pads and tiny nails,
Anus and tail
Left by a predator fleeing predation.

Middle Ground or Extremes, which will it be?
I can grant your preference, with the almighty
Null powers vested in me.

Evanescent

She barks in the yard when I leave her at home.
Should I quicken my pace or slow it down?
She's a whippet mixed with some huge hound
A whippet when running; she stots, she bounds.

With big hound sound she barks today.
Do our neighbors complain? They might, they may.
Both perturbed and resolute I walk on,
Her sound waves spread over West Side lawns.

The Doppler Effect, now I'm out of range
New thoughts bound back from an earlier stage.
Yellow school bus looms, takes me in, shifts gears,
My house grows smaller then disappears.

Is it still there? Is my mother inside?
I'm Bishop Berkeley's daughter on this ride.

If I Were A Yankee And You Were The Moon

If I were a Yankee and you were the Moon
I'd still wake beside you, we just wouldn't know.
Nor if it was you, your effortless pull
That burdens my throws.
Runner not out, but just by a step—that means he's in.
Or is it an effort, even for you?
But one so accustomed, gracefully smooth.
Orbit after orbit after orbit—all just as one.

If I were a Yankee and you were the Moon
I'd practice my change-up, my slider, my curve
My split fingered fastball, two seams and four.
In the rotation, I'd want
You around us
Me touched by you.
But who'd cut the grass, and who'd make it grow?
When would be safe? And what would be home?

Future Tense

Will she (please) respond to me tonight, tomorrow, Now?
Will her news be good?
Will I feel relieved or stressed? Or both? Or like a fool?

When I learn, will I feel drained, even if elated?
Will I feel somewhat less alive, different from when I waited?

Waiting is a graceless state, full of future tense,
    A captured now
    Depleted past
Both linked by fragile suture.
    A hopeless hopeful unforeseen
    Inevitable
    Tense future.

World

1.   The world is too big.
I don't understand it.
I'll get me a car
To travel some miles
To make things seem smaller
More familiar to me.

2.   The world is too small.
I can't quite observe it.
I'll get me some glasses
To see objects better
To make things seem bigger
More familiar to me.

3.   The world is too complex.
I don't seem to grasp it.
I'll get me some books
To teach me some wisdom
To make things seem clearer
More familiar to me.

* * * * * * * * * * * * * * *

4.   Time is too long,
Routine so boring
From five to twenty
Takes hundreds of years.

* * * * * * * * * * * * *

5. My world is too cold.
    I can stand it no longer.
    I'll take me a lover
    To give heat and succor
    To make life feel warmer
    More sustaining for me.

6. My world is too busy.
    Can't manage, can't cope.
    I'll buy me a smart phone
     To do more more quickly
     To make things seem easy
    More accomplished by me.

7. My world is too dark.
    I don't see my shadow.
    I'll find me a comet
    To light up the way
    To make things more sparkly
    More brilliance from me.

* * * * * * * * * * * * *

8. Ah, Time is too short
    Life rife with drama
    From twenty to seventy
    Takes only one year.

* * * * * * * * * *

Our world is so simple.
There's just living   Just living and dying
Not much (so much) in between.

Section VIII: An Everyday Tragedy

A Death in the Family

Betty

Betty was tall.
Basketball tall.
She was the center
We circled around her,
The rest of the team.
She pivoted gracefully
She made you the center.
And you were
When you were.

She played the slots.
Early big winnings
Masses of merchandize
Mammoth debt.

Basketball could have been her game
Were she born in '66.

Golf: Awkward, cumbersome game
Unnatural motions,
Rendered lovely
By Betty
The natural athlete.

She played as well as her very practiced
High achieving and exacting sister
And as well as her *male* older sibling,

Did she ever practice?

Mutations: Random but (Usually) Bad

Tall people have more cells
More cells
Accumulate more mutations
More cancers.
Betty worked night shifts
At the casino...
More cancers
Confused bio-rhythms.
Stress shortens telomeres (caps on genes)
More cancers.
Leukemia.

The Surprising Comforts of Arithmetic

i

I was afraid of that disease
So afraid
I was afraid of the word.

In the subway
I would not sit under
An advertisement:
A family in a glass frame
With the glass shattered
Over the victim.

The ad's clock
Had months instead of minutes.
Nine months,
Nine months to kill,
Nine months from diagnosis to death.
Nine months
To bring new life.

I played
Arithmetic games.
What if they waited to tell the doctors?
Would the clock start later?
Would they have more months
To beat leukemia?

"Square Burger,"
Promised "Four Bites More"
More than any round burger.
What if I could eat it in four bites or less?
What if a patient
Lasted longer than nine months?
Wrong diagnosis?
No leukemia.

The Dangers of Geometry

After the stem cell transplant
The rest of her life
Was a triangular struggle
Infection vs.
Transplant reaction vs.
Leukemic return,
Three against one
Against Betty.

The Surprising Comforts of Arithmetic

ii

Three against one and
Betty lost.
It was in not-yet Summer:
One year after the transplant remission,
Three and a half years after the diagnosis

Sixty-five years
In a life expectancy of seventy-eight.
—83.333%—
This irrational number has allowed
The cold but real comfort
Only real numbers can bring.

Betty's Things

Betty without her things felt lonely.
Overstuffed rooms with too big furniture,
Unwrapped sweaters, unworn pants,
Barely ridden bicycles,
Indoor exercise equipment,
Paintings, framed, unframed, never-to-be hung
Cookware and electric appliances, expensive
Colorful collections.

Sat pitiful, tiny and alone in the Goodwill van.

Her things survived her
Forlorn, scattered
Without a home
Like words in exile,
Banished from poems.

Section IX: Coda—An End to "Everyday"

Poem of Our Pandemic
Monday March 30, 2020

I. Hear Here

There are positive cases
Here, we hear.
One Hundred Seven.

II. Alone Together

Six feet away   we stay.
Everyone the carrier
Everyone the victim
Hearty Healthy Hello
My fellow fellow!

III. Walking Up the Hills on a Weekday Morning

Whose hills these are
I know them well
I go up fast
But down is slow.

It's cold today
Should I return to Go
Now?

No
Someone's car has moved
Wow!

Oh, that's where the Wheaten Terrier lives!
Kids throwing a frisbee
Will they move
Or?
Shall I leave the beaten path
To pursue the path
Of resistance?

A robin. In that yard
Hopping one small yard (not two) from me.
But this is not bird flu
It's our pandemic.
       Steep Hill
       Steep Hill
       Steep Hill
       Steep Hill
Small changes
Not as profound
As I pretended.
Nature goes on
We are up-ended.

Tuesday March 31, 2020

IV. Numbers

Today positive case number is
One Hundred Sixty-Seven
How often are they prime numbers?
Positive is so negative
Would that they were imaginary numbers

V. Flowers that Bloom in the Spring, Tra-La

Forty degrees
Feels like thirty five
Flowers bloom on
Yes, yes, yes
Violet and yellow, pink and white
In denial? Uncaring about our angst?
Immune.
When in danger
Plants communicate
Chemically
Dog whistling
But not to me

What color is the Covid-19 (prime number) virus?
Lovely, with its spikey corona
Google, google scholar what do you say?

Ask your smart speaker
since it's so smart

Ask if you will get the virus
Ask how bad will it be
Ask if you will die, and then as a test
Ask if.

Sunday April 19, 2020

VI. Numbers Revisited

Report to Faculty: University of Michigan Hospital

April 1:	162 positive cases	
April 4	185 positive cases	14 discharged to home. (Deaths not reported.)
April 6	224 positive cases	8 discharged to home. (No deaths reported.)
April 7	216 positive cases	16 discharged to home.
April 8	225 positive cases	
April 9	232 positive cases	Tornado warnings.
April 10	234 positive cases	15 discharged to home. 0 deaths.
April 11	218 positive cases	20 discharged to home. (No deaths reported)
April 12	213 positive cases	6 discharged to home. 6 deaths.
April 13	220 positive cases	5 discharged to home. 2 deaths.
April 14	221 positive cases	5 discharged to home. (No deaths reported.)

April 15	227 positive cases	13 discharged to home. 2 deaths.
April 16	232 positive cases	18 discharged to home. 1 death.
April 17	203 positive cases	17 discharged to home. 3 deaths.
April 18	209 positive cases	20 discharged (some (?) to skilled nursing; excludes hospices).
April 19	199 positive cases	8 discharged to home. 6 deaths.

Positives are negative. Some data not free for release.

Prime numbered cases: just two-twenty-three.

Tornadoes, recorded, a distraction

Deaths, only whisper

The saddest subtractions.

Thursday April 23, 2020

VII. All the News is Covid

All the news is Covid
The politicians livid

The globe infected
Cases undetected
Many unprotected

Unmerrily we roll

Suspended animation
Awaiting vaccination
Is this a forced vacation?

Others born to toil
On our unfair soil.

Wednesday May 6, 2020

VIII. The Wisdom of Dogs: A Sonnet

I know how dogs tell time
    Follow increase in scent
    Pattern derived from
    Where the prey went

I know why dogs tell time
       Pattern derived from
       Where the prey was
       Sure to establish
       Where prey goes

Humans are harder to read
       We bob
       We weave
       We truth tell
       Deceive

Our masks are in place
To cover de-face

Thursday, May 28, 2020

IX. Four Leaf Clover

A year far from both pandemics
Nineteen Hundred Fifty-Three
Nursery school looms
Frightens me.

Dad says: let's find a 4-leaf clover
For good luck, a good luck omen.
Try we did, but soon gave up.
No preschool prize for us.

Two Thousand Nineteen
Months before we met young Covid
Instructions for *trace-tracking* 4-leaf clovers
We had seen—
Frivolity in the Sunday magazine.

Innocence lasts as long as she can
Flames and sparks until she's out.
Flames and sparks until she's over.
With or without a 4-leaf clover.